Contents

Sails—The Story of Ships 7
    Early Ships 8
    Today's Ships 16
    Special Ships 20
    We've Come A Long Way 26

Rails—The Story of Trains 29
    Early Trains 30
    Today's Trains 36
    Special Trains 40
    Tomorrow's Trains 46

Wings—The Story of Planes 49
    Early Planes 51
    Today's Planes 58
    Special Planes 64
    We've Come A Long Way 69

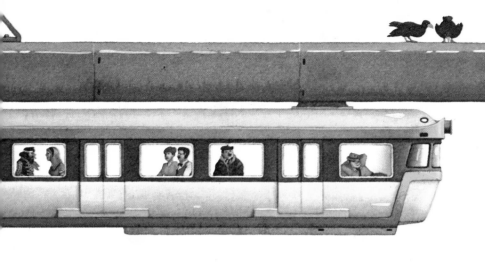

SAILS, RAILS AND WINGS

By Seymour Reit

Pictures by Roberto Innocenti

Golden Press • New York
Western Publishing Company, Inc.
Racine, Wisconsin

SAILS

The Story of Ships

Rocks and waterfalls were problems for early river sailors.

EARLY SHIPS

No one knows for sure, but the story of how ships were invented may go like this: Long, long ago, long before there were roads or trains or planes, a weary traveler was walking beside a river. Then a log floated by. The walker climbed onto the log, and rode the rest of the way home. This floating log was probably the very first "ship."

Later on people learned to hollow out the logs, so they could sit in them and paddle. Some early sailors tied logs together with vines to form rafts. Others made boats with the skin of a large animal. They stretched the skin over a frame of tree branches.

Early boats were made by chopping up the inside of a log with a stone ax. Boats made this way are called dugouts.

Next people put sails on their ships. When the wind blew, it filled the sails and pushed the ships. Early sailboats could only go in the direction in which the wind was blowing. And if the wind blew too hard, or not hard enough, or in the wrong direction, rowers went to work. Other people were needed to steer the ships.

As time passed, bigger ships were built and more sails were added. People studied the wind and placed the sails to catch every breeze. These bigger sailboats could travel on long voyages—even without the help of any rowers.

The first sailboats were made thousands of years ago in Egypt.

This ship was used to ram an enemy's vessel. Rowers had to row to a rhythm beat out on a drum.

Sailing warships had many decks, which bristled with cannons. In rough seas the lowest gunports were closed so water wouldn't flood the ship.

The Vikings were expert sailors. They explored many lands. Some people think they discovered America before Columbus.

Columbus sailed for 2½ months to get from Europe to the Americas. His small wooden ship the *Santa Maria* looked like this.

SãoDomingo

The *Mayflower* carried settlers to America. Its average speed was only 2 miles per hour. Most people walk faster than that!

Pirate ships prowled the seas hoping to capture vessels with valuable cargo. Sometimes the pirates sank a captured ship.

Sailing ships that were wide and bulky ruled the seas for hundreds of years. They were used to fight battles, explore unknown waters, and carry passengers and cargo all over the world.

Then a new kind of sailing ship came into use. It was long and narrow. It had taller masts with extra sails. It could speed through the waves much faster than the old-style ships. This new kind of ship was called a clipper ship. It was the fastest sailing ship ever made.

Graceful clipper ships sailed from America to faraway places like Australia and China. Their Captains took pride in setting new port-to-port speed records. The *Sea Witch* was a China clipper famous for swiftness.

Another fast sailing ship in the time of the clippers was the schooner. This one was nearly 400 feet long and had sails on 7 tall masts.

Like most early steamships, the *Clermont* also had sails. It was the first successful steam-powered passenger ship.

The *Great Eastern* was the biggest ship of its time. It could carry thousands of passengers.

CHARLOTTE

Flat-bottomed paddle-wheel steamers rode up and down shallow rivers.

The warship *Monitor* was steam powered. It was one of the first ships with metal sides.

America's first working steamboat was built in 1807 by Robert Fulton. In those days people laughed at the idea of steam engines for ships. Fulton named his vessel the *Clermont,* but everyone else called it "Fulton's Folly."

Ships powered by steam engines soon put the wind-powered sailing ships out of business. Steamships could travel faster than sailships, but more important, they could travel anytime. At long last sailors did not have to wait for the wind to blow. They went whenever they wanted—wind or no wind.

TODAY'S SHIPS

Today there are boats and ships of all shapes and sizes. They do many useful jobs. Some carry mail. Some, like ferryboats and ocean liners, carry passengers. Fishing boats bring in tons of fish to help feed people. Cargo ships and tankers go to distant ports to pick up or deliver many things people use every day, like cars and clothes and oil and oats.

Dock cranes move cargo from ships to waiting railroad trains.

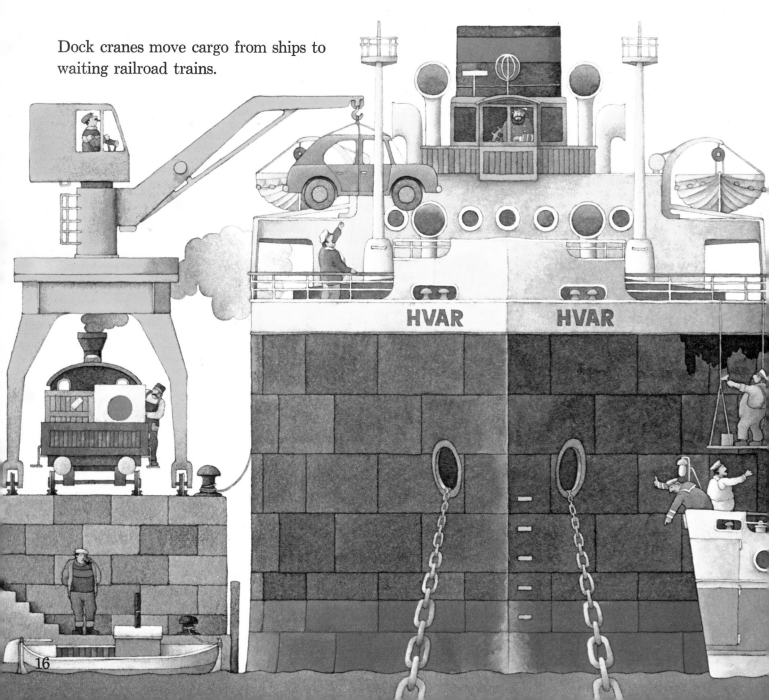

Ocean liners are like floating cities. They have shops, libraries, movie theaters, indoor pools, and beauty parlors.

This is a trawler. It drags a strong fishing net along the sea bottom.

Some people ride ferryboats to school or work each day, just as others take cars, buses, or trains.

ARLÖ

Lighthouses help ships find their way safely.
They are like traffic signs for water travelers.

passenger ship

patrol boat

ferryboat

fireboat

motorboat

A harbor is a busy place. And a crowded one. Passenger liners steam in after long ocean crossings. Ferryboats shuttle back and forth. Barges load and unload at piers. Fireboats, police boats, tugboats, and cargo ships are everywhere. All sailors have to learn special "traffic rules" of the sea. This makes water travel safer. Just think what harbor traffic jams there might be if sailors didn't have any "rules of the road"!

oil tanker

sailboat

cargo ship

barge

sight-seeing boat

tugboat

In some places people live year round on houseboats. They take their homes with them whenever they move.

SPECIAL SHIPS

Different parts of the world have their own special ships. In Venice, a city in Italy that has many canals, gondolas are pushed through the water with long poles. The people of the West Indies travel from one island to another in sturdy catamarans. The Eskimos of the Far North ride in special canoes called kayaks. Kayaks fit snugly around the rider's waist so the cold Arctic waters don't get in.

Tourists sight-seeing in a gondola

Catamarans look like
2 boats joined together.
The twin hulls make these
boats hard to sink.

Did you ever see a ship travel *above* the water?
The hovercraft does. It floats on a cushion of air.
Hydrofoils can also skim above the water's surface.
They speed along on metal fins.

Propellers move the hovercraft forward.
It has a rubber "skirt" that fills with
air. It can go over water or land!

A hydrofoil ride is faster and smoother
than that of a ship whose hull sits in
the water.

Today's nuclear-powered submarines
can go around the world underwater.

Other ships move silently beneath the sea. In bathyspheres, bathyscaphes, and submarines, scientists study the dark and mysterious undersea world. With these ships people have been able to dive deep into places they've never seen before.

A bathysphere is attached by a cable to a surface ship. A bathyscaphe moves about under its own power.

America's first submarine could stay underwater half an hour. It was hand cranked by a single crew member.

Rushing the white-water rapids in kayaks

Iceboating on a frozen lake

Many boats are just for fun and sport. Water skiers are pulled by fast motorboats. Snorkelers and skin divers use boats to take them to coral reefs. Racers compete in speedboats and sailboats. Campers enjoy canoe trips. And some people like rowboats for just sitting and bobbing lazily up and down in the waves.

Fishing from a rowboat or paddling in a canoe is fun to do with friends.

Racing the wind in a sleek speedboat

Relaxing on board a yacht

Sailing in a strong breeze takes skill.

Viewing the undersea world —and being viewed

NEPTUNE II

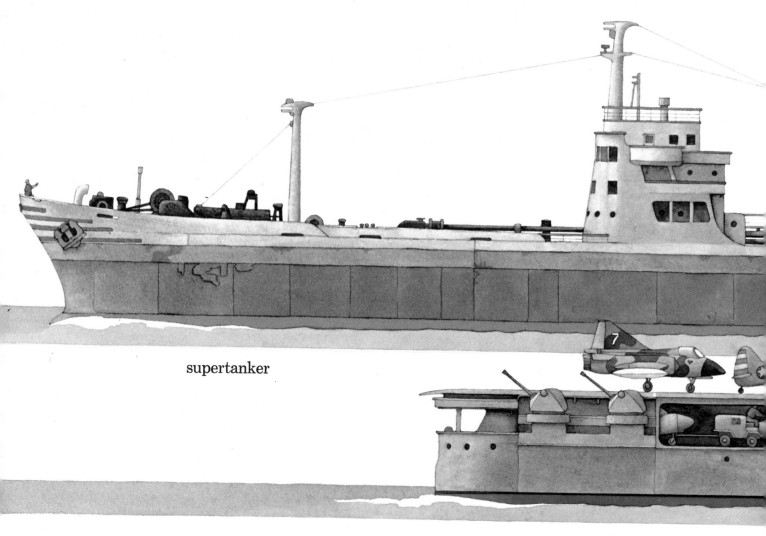

supertanker

aircraft carrier

WE'VE COME A LONG WAY

People and ships have changed a lot since the first floating log was ridden down a river. We have gone from crude rafts to modern hovercrafts, from tiny sailing ships to huge aircraft carriers, from slow paddleboats to speedy ocean liners.

It's hard to imagine that ships will ever be better than the ones we have today. But the people in Columbus' time may have thought the same thing, and just look how far ships have come since then!

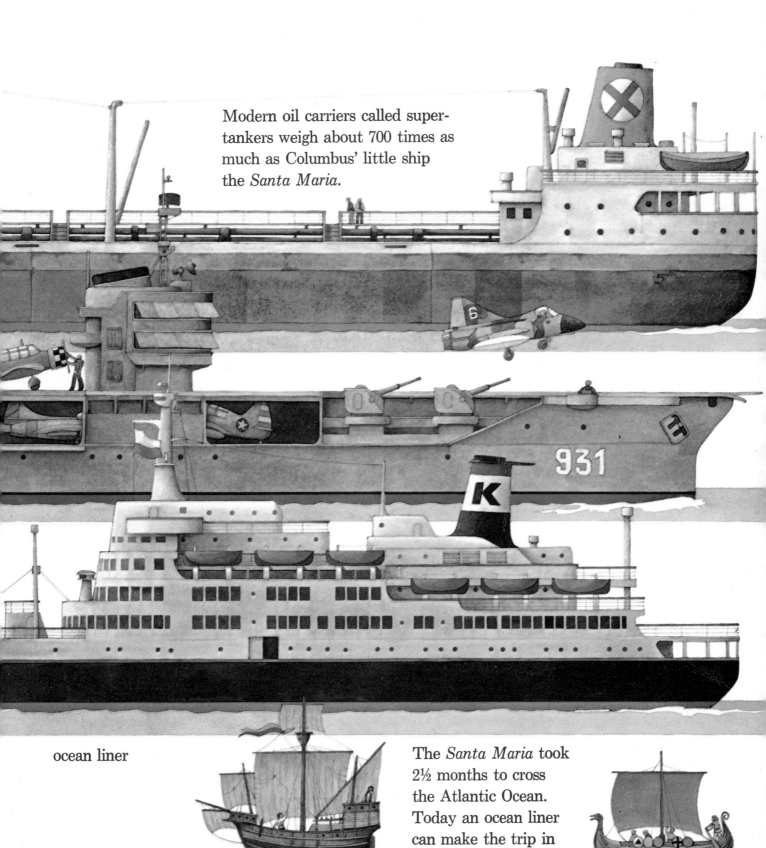

Modern oil carriers called super-
tankers weigh about 700 times as
much as Columbus' little ship
the *Santa Maria*.

ocean liner

The *Santa Maria* took
2½ months to cross
the Atlantic Ocean.
Today an ocean liner
can make the trip in
5½ days.

Columbus' *Santa Maria*

Viking ship

RAILS
The Story of Trains

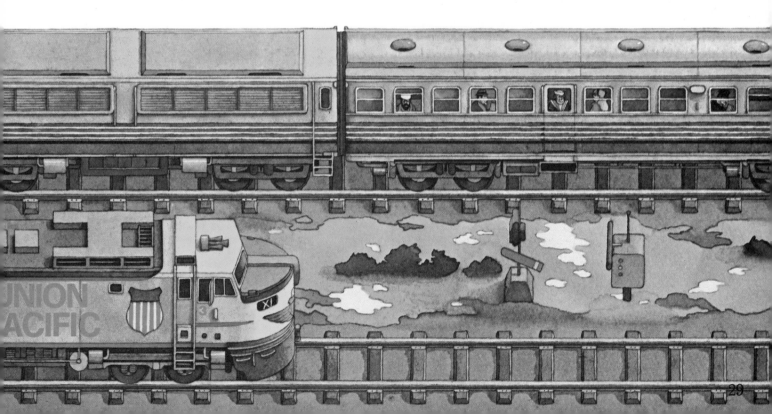

EARLY TRAINS

Many years ago, miners were digging for coal deep under the ground. They piled the coal into wagons that stood on tracks. Then they pushed and pulled to get the wagons out of the mine.

These coal-wagon trains with their wooden tracks were the first railroads. But the real story of railways began with the invention of the locomotive steam engine.

Mine floors were rough and uneven. The wheels and rails made it easier to do the hard work of moving the heavy wagons.

6

Sometimes tracks went from a mine to a
nearby town. Horses were used to pull the
coal trains along these "tramways."

Early railway passengers made short
trips in horse-drawn carriages.

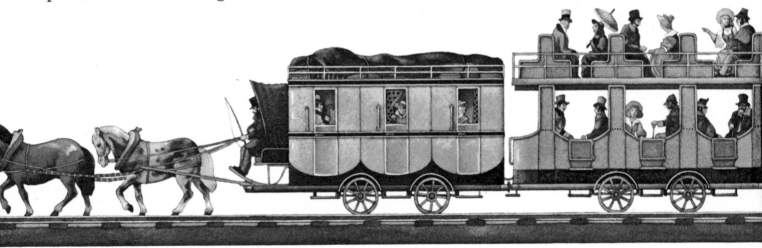

After the steam engine was invented,
trains could move on their own power.
And the locomotives did not need to
stop for a rest the way horses did.

The first steam-powered locomotives were built about 170 years ago, in England and America. They were quite the sight to see! Smoke and burning cinders showered out of tall smokestacks. The small engines chugged along noisily. Some people scoffed at these strange new machines, calling them "tea kettles on wheels." But most people saw that locomotives really did work—and were fascinated by them.

One of the first steam engines ever built was the *Catch Me Who Can*. It only went about 12 miles per hour. The little engine was displayed in London, England, as an amusement attraction. People came from miles away to pay for a ride or to just sneak a peek.

Here's how a steam engine works: Coal or wood is burned in a firebox. The fire heats water stored in a boiler. When the water boils it turns into steam, just as it does in a whistling tea kettle. The steam rushes through pipes to the pistons. It pushes the pistons back and forth. The pumping pistons move a rod that turns the wheels. The wheels move the engine, and the engine pulls the train.

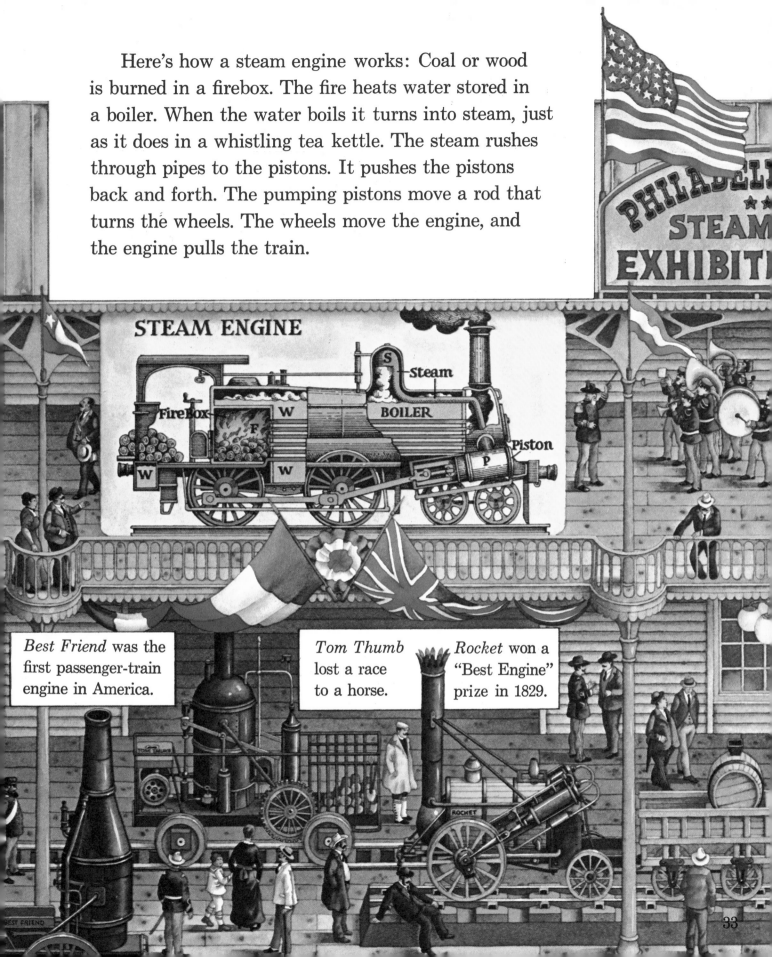

PHILADEL
STEAM
EXHIBIT

STEAM ENGINE

Steam

FireBox

BOILER

Piston

Best Friend was the first passenger-train engine in America.

Tom Thumb lost a race to a horse.

Rocket won a "Best Engine" prize in 1829.

One of the greatest adventures in railroading took place when Americans built the first transcontinental rail line. Two companies competed for 5 years to lay the most tracks. They worked toward each other, one coming from the East and one coming from the West. Then, in 1869, the tracks met. A golden spike was used to fasten the final rail.

Names of rail officials are on the golden spike.

At the golden spike ceremony, May 1869

Sometimes cattle wandered onto the tracks. Locomotives had big iron bumpers called cow catchers to keep the tracks clear.

Trains kept getting bigger and faster. And more comfortable. A man named George Pullman built a dining car where meals were served. He also built a car with beds, so that people could sleep on long trips. The beds, called berths, folded back into seats in the daytime.

Some people had private railroad cars. They hooked them up to regular trains when they took trips.

CHICAGO Railway Pullman C

DINING CAR

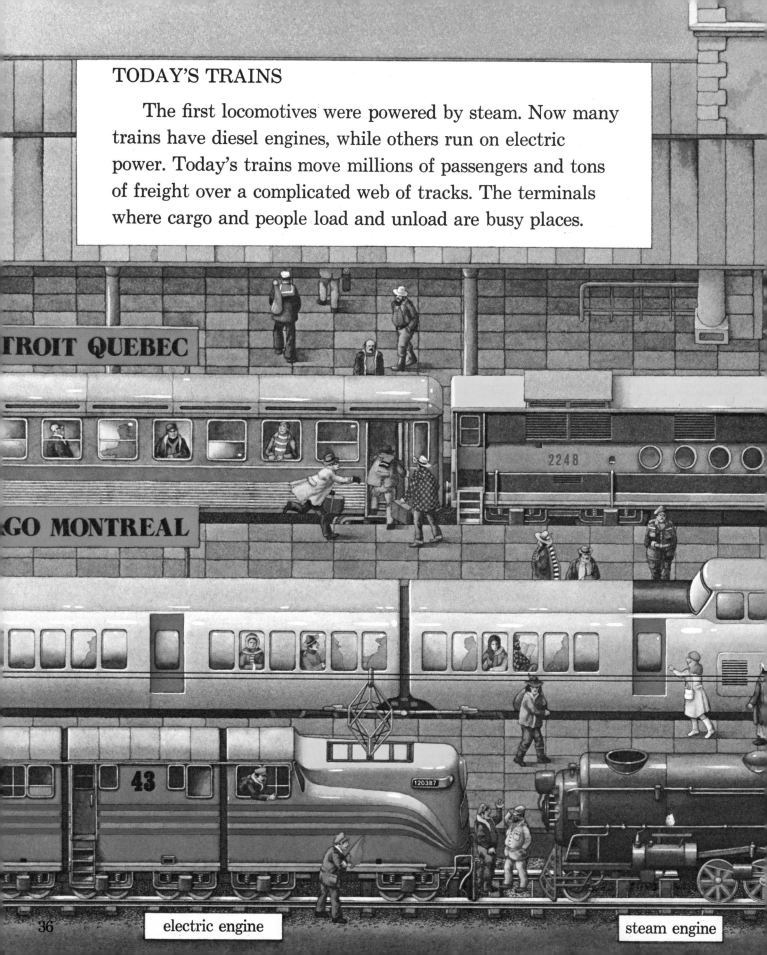

TODAY'S TRAINS

The first locomotives were powered by steam. Now many trains have diesel engines, while others run on electric power. Today's trains move millions of passengers and tons of freight over a complicated web of tracks. The terminals where cargo and people load and unload are busy places.

TROIT QUEBEC

GO MONTREAL

2248

43

120387

electric engine

steam engine

electric engine

diesel-electric engine

gas-turbine engine

St LOUIS BOSTON

GW 4399

P 42
O NERE N

17
30

S

37

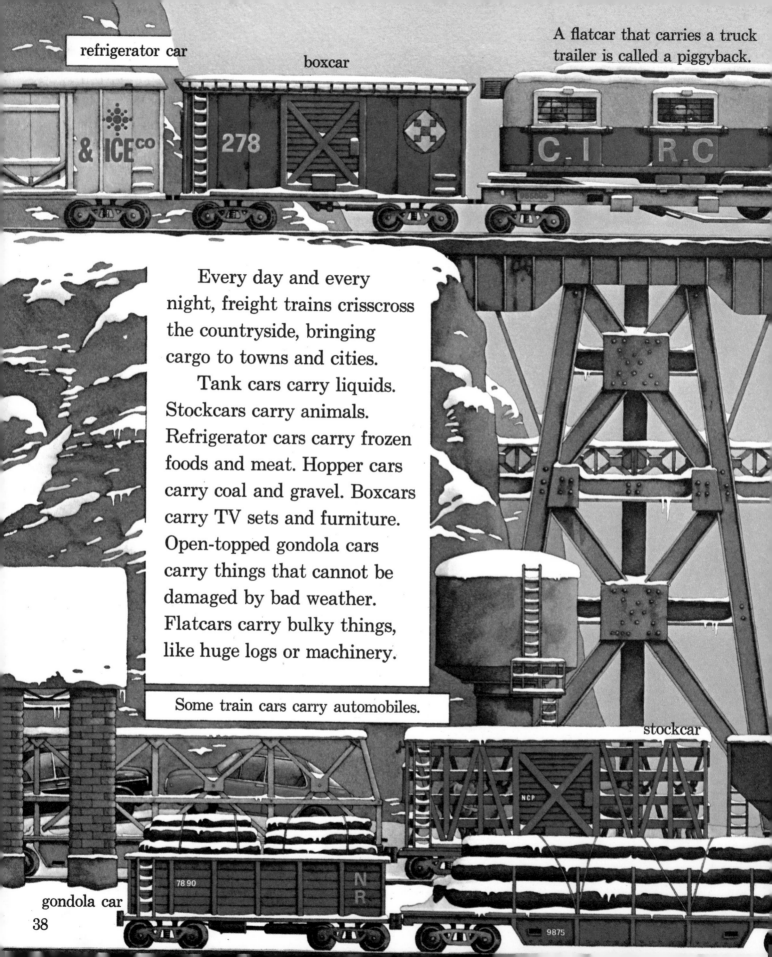

refrigerator car

boxcar

A flatcar that carries a truck trailer is called a piggyback.

&ICE CO

278

C.I R.C

Every day and every night, freight trains crisscross the countryside, bringing cargo to towns and cities.

Tank cars carry liquids. Stockcars carry animals. Refrigerator cars carry frozen foods and meat. Hopper cars carry coal and gravel. Boxcars carry TV sets and furniture. Open-topped gondola cars carry things that cannot be damaged by bad weather. Flatcars carry bulky things, like huge logs or machinery.

Some train cars carry automobiles.

stockcar

NCP

gondola car

78 90

N R

9875

engines

hopper car

flatcar

tank car

The train's last car is the
caboose, an office for the crew.

SPECIAL TRAINS

In places with high mountains, cogwheel trains are often used. These trains have special toothed wheels, which fit into special toothed tracks. The cogwheels keep the trains from slipping on steep slopes.

Cable cars are also used in mountainous areas. They make it possible to get from one high place to another.

The "teeth" on a cogwheel mesh with the track in somewhat the same way as the "teeth" of a zipper lock together.

Cable cars hang from metal
ropes attached to high towers.

Trolleys moved by cables are
sometimes used in cities with
especially hilly streets.

One New York subway
car can weigh 43 tons.

People in big cities often live far from where they work and shop. They need a way of getting from place to place quickly and easily. Some cities have special trains to help.

City trains that run on tracks built high above the ground are called elevated trains, or "els." The world's first elevated railroad was built in New York City in 1867.

Other city trains, called subways, travel in tunnels under the ground. Some subways are so far below the surface that passengers have to take an elevator or escalator to get to the train station! Hundreds of miles of subway tracks run beneath the city buildings.

There are subways in New York, Paris, London, Moscow, Tokyo, and other big cities. Millions of people ride in them every day. If there were no subways in these places, the streets would be jammed with honking cars and buses.

In Paris some subway trains move quietly on rubber tires.

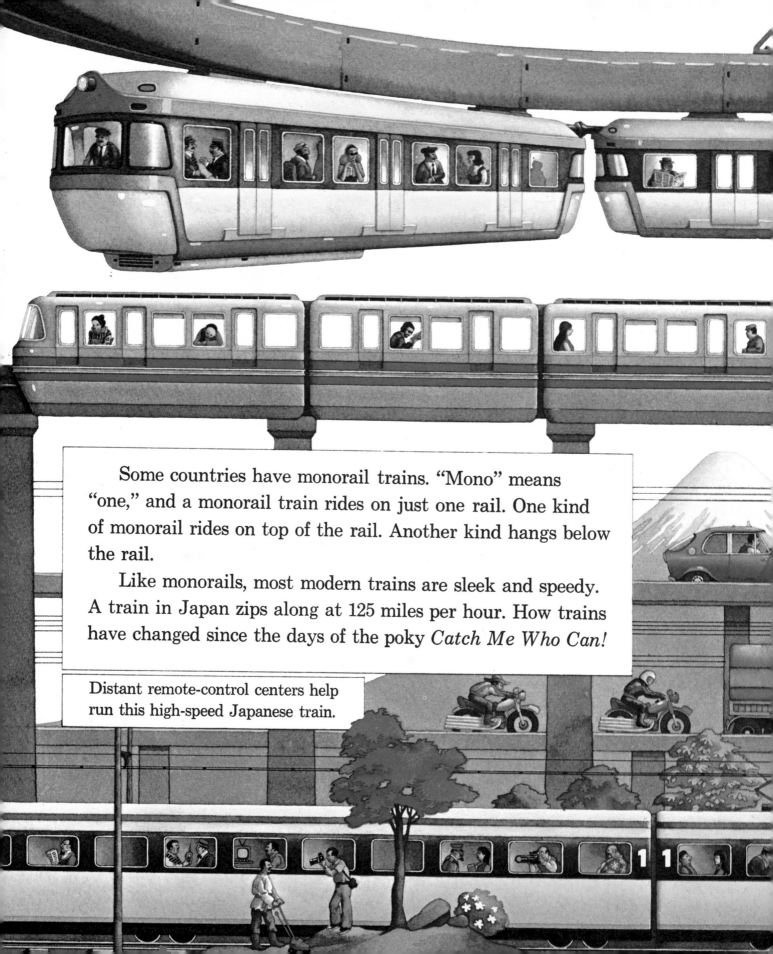

Some countries have monorail trains. "Mono" means "one," and a monorail train rides on just one rail. One kind of monorail rides on top of the rail. Another kind hangs below the rail.

Like monorails, most modern trains are sleek and speedy. A train in Japan zips along at 125 miles per hour. How trains have changed since the days of the poky *Catch Me Who Can!*

Distant remote-control centers help run this high-speed Japanese train.

Riding a monorail that hangs
below the rail feels almost
like being in an airplane.

This monorail balances on
top of the rail.

45

TOMORROW'S TRAINS

What will the trains of tomorrow be like? You can be sure they will be faster and more comfortable than ever.

Future trains will use new kinds of power. Some locomotives will have jet engines like those on airplanes. Others may have atomic engines. These new trains will all be fast moving to keep up with tomorrow's fast-moving world. Just think, someday you may travel in one of these rocketlike express trains.

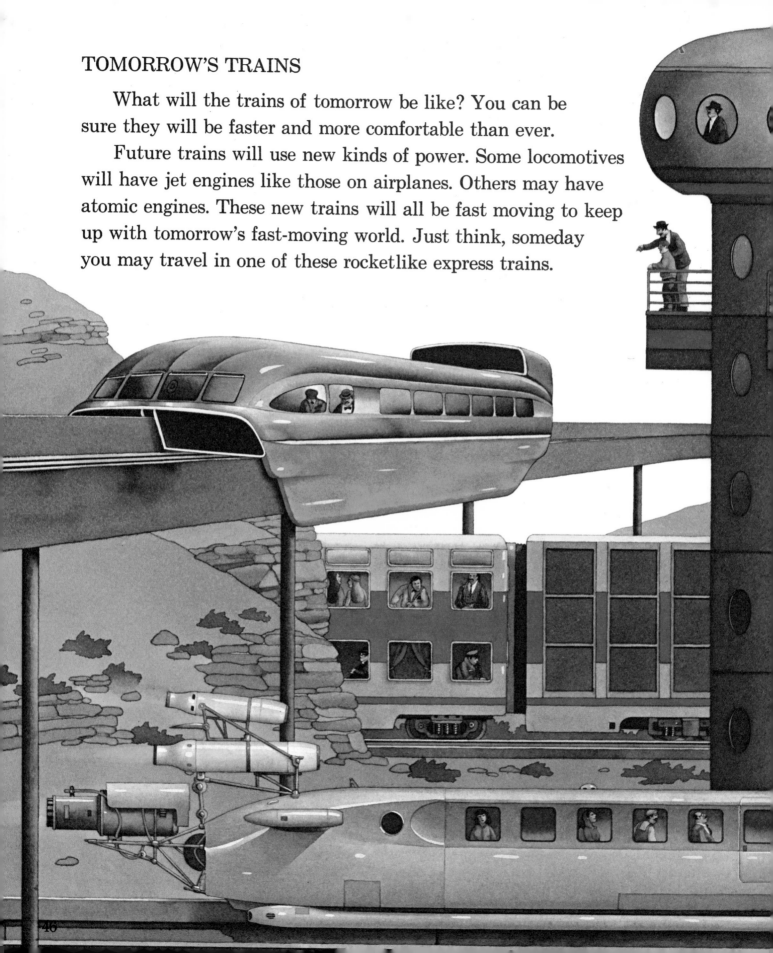

Monorails high in the air may take the place of trains on the ground. The land the tracks were on may be used for farms, homes, or roads.

AEROTRAIN 230

Future trains may have atomic engines like this test model.

Jet-powered locomotives are being tried out in France.

WINGS

The Story of Planes

The first people to try to fly used homemade wings, but wing flapping was strictly for the birds!

A great thinker named Leonardo Da Vinci drew sketches for flying machines 500 years ago. He did this after he had studied how birds fly. He also had ideas for a parachute and a helicopter. But the machines he planned were never built.

A flying machine designed to look like this was thought of by a scientist around 1670.

A glider has no power of its own. It is carried by the wind. On breezeless days it can't fly at all.

This balloon was filled with a lighter-than-air gas called hydrogen. The flier tried to steer with a sail.

Early balloons were filled with heated air, which made them rise.

EARLY PLANES

People have always dreamed of being able to fly, but for many years no one knew how. Early experimenters built wings and tied them to their arms, hoping to fly like birds. Scientists drew sketches of flying machines and thought about "sky boats" steered by "air paddles." But only about 200 years ago did people begin to fly at last. The first fliers went up in balloons and in giant kites called gliders.

the Wright brothers

Count slowly: 1...2...3...
4...5...6...7...8...9...10...
11...12. That is how long the
first airplane flight lasted—
just 12 seconds!

That first flight took place in
1903, in America. The fliers, Wilbur and Orville Wright,
were brothers. They were the first ones ever to fly and
control a powered flying machine. And on that day in 1903,
they changed the future of the world.

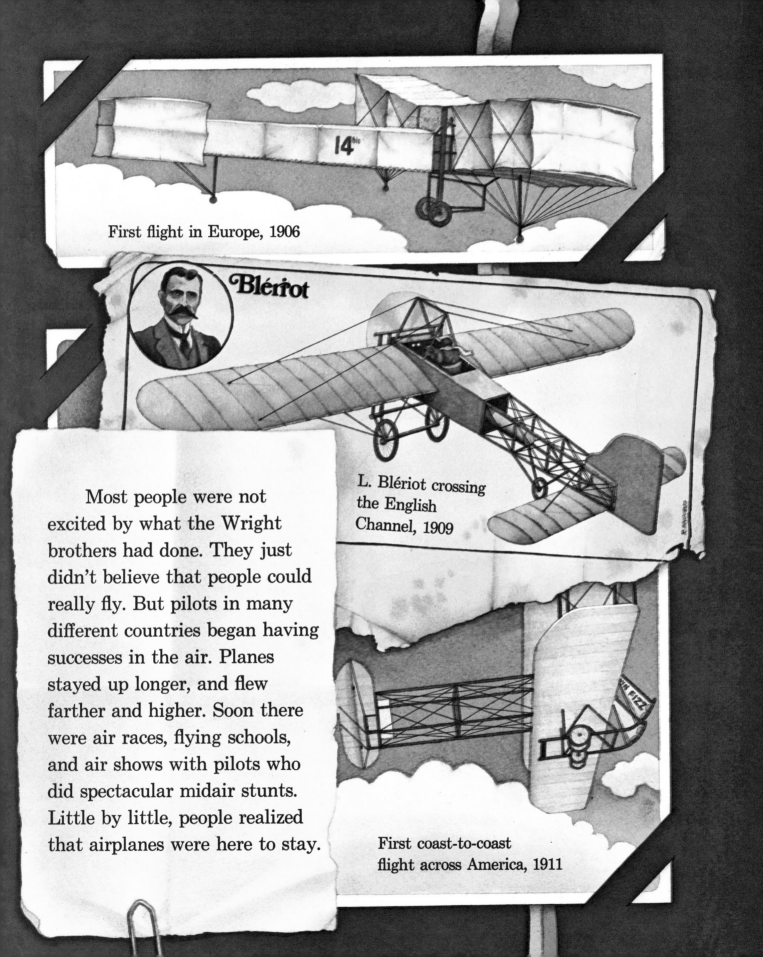

First flight in Europe, 1906

Blériot

L. Blériot crossing
the English
Channel, 1909

Most people were not
excited by what the Wright
brothers had done. They just
didn't believe that people could
really fly. But pilots in many
different countries began having
successes in the air. Planes
stayed up longer, and flew
farther and higher. Soon there
were air races, flying schools,
and air shows with pilots who
did spectacular midair stunts.
Little by little, people realized
that airplanes were here to stay.

First coast-to-coast
flight across America, 1911

When the airplane was still a very new invention and most people thought it was only good for circus stunts, a great World War broke out. The airplane's first practical job was as a weapon. It was used for spying and fighting, while airships called dirigibles were sometimes used for bombing. Many pilots became war heroes.

After the war, pilots continued to do brave deeds. One of the most famous pilots ever was Charles Lindbergh. He flew across the vast Atlantic Ocean—by himself! No one had ever done that before. He flew 3,600 miles. It took nearly 34 hours. When he arrived in France, a huge crowd of people carried him on their shoulders. "Lucky Lindy" was a hero.

Amelia Earhart was another famous pilot. She became known for her daring long-distance flights.

Caproni
(Italy)

Spad (France)

Sopwith Camel
(Great Britain)

Amazed fishermen spied Lindbergh's plane as he flew across the Atlantic. Most of them had never seen an airplane before.

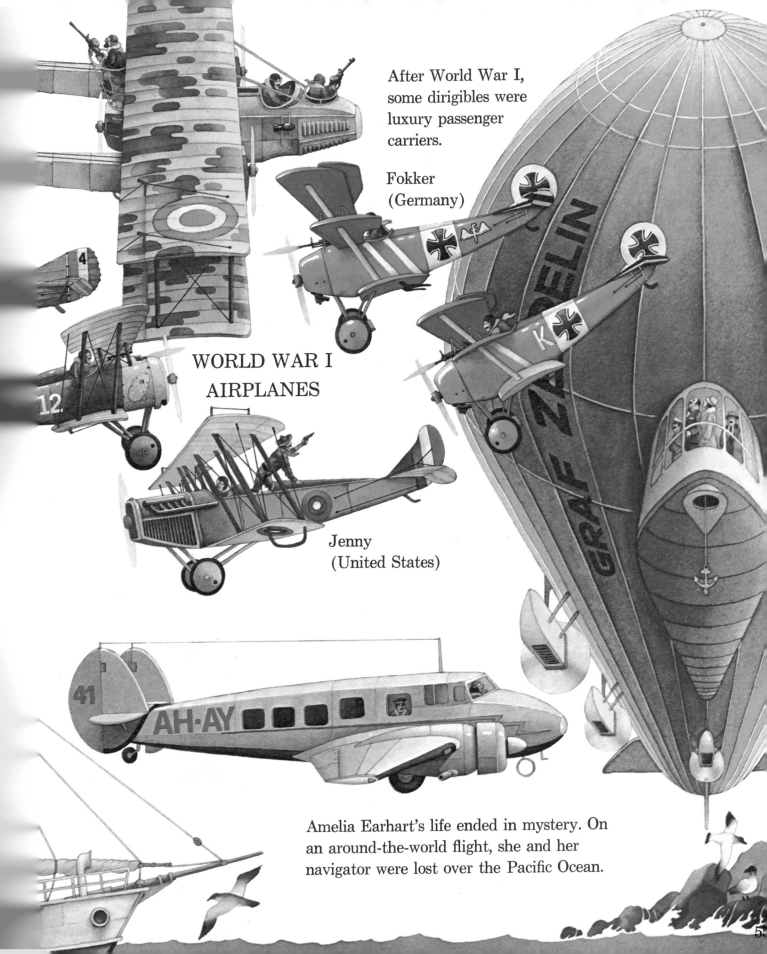

After World War I, some dirigibles were luxury passenger carriers.

Fokker
(Germany)

WORLD WAR I
AIRPLANES

Jenny
(United States)

Amelia Earhart's life ended in mystery. On an around-the-world flight, she and her navigator were lost over the Pacific Ocean.

After Lindbergh's famous flight, changes came fast. More powerful airplanes were built, and longer flights were possible. Now planes were made of metal, instead of wood and cloth. More and more airplanes were used to carry freight and mail. Special planes just for passengers were built. People began to visit parts of the world they hadn't been able to reach before. Airplanes made the world seem smaller.

Zero (Japan)

With this plane, passengers traveled quickly, safely, and comfortably for the first time.

Giant seaplanes carried passengers, freight, or mail across the oceans.

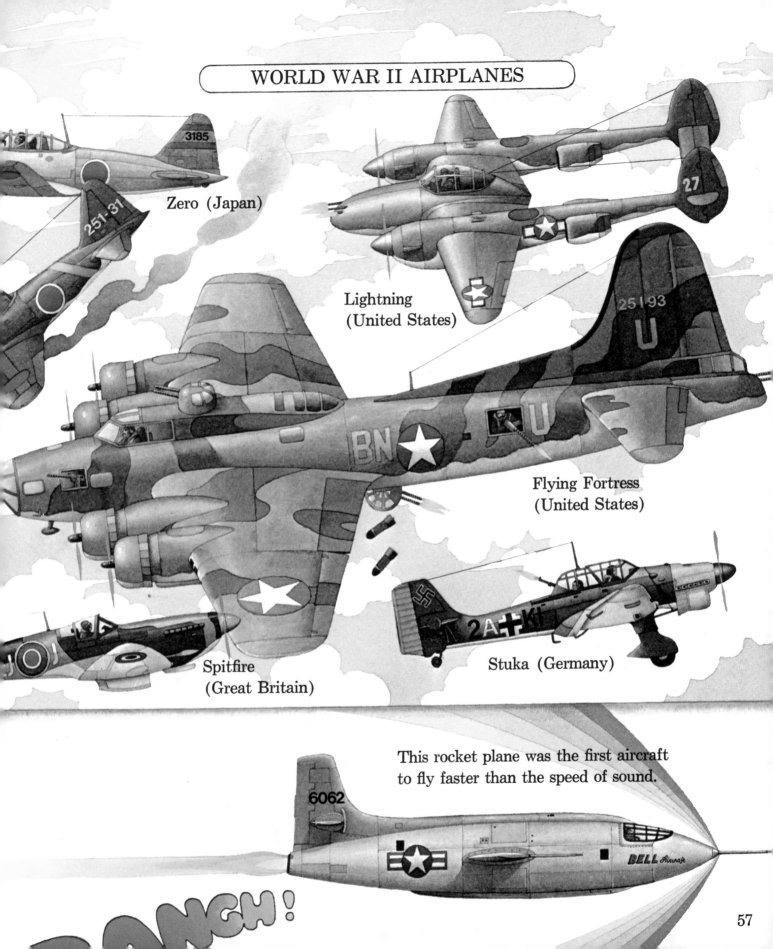

WORLD WAR II AIRPLANES

Zero (Japan)

Lightning
(United States)

Flying Fortress
(United States)

Spitfire
(Great Britain)

Stuka (Germany)

This rocket plane was the first aircraft
to fly faster than the speed of sound.

TODAY'S PLANES

A modern airport is a very busy place. Every few minutes, a plane takes off or lands. Now another flight is about to leave. The fuel tanks are filled, and the engines have been checked. Passengers and baggage are on board. The crew looks over the instruments.

When all is ready, the Captain taxis the plane to the runway, and waits. At last the control tower sends the message: "You are cleared for takeoff!" And another flight zooms on its way.

helicopter

Boeing 727

Douglas DC-10

Fokker F-27

Boeing 737

Boeing 707

Douglas DC-8

FLUGHAFEN

Today there are many kinds of planes, and they do many different jobs. Some are "flying gas stations." They refuel smaller planes in midair. Others are cargo carriers. They take goods and products all over the world. Some of these sky freighters can haul more than 300,000 pounds. This equals the weight of 50 elephants!

Giant cargo freighters are sometimes called flying boxcars. They carry everything from baby chicks to trucks and tanks.

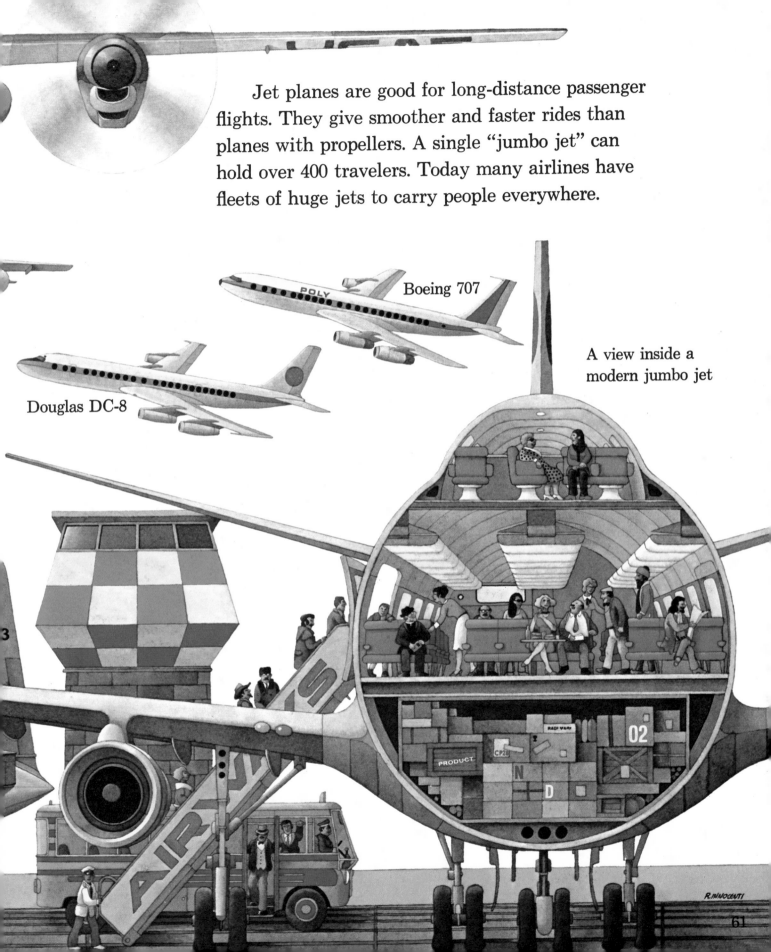

Jet planes are good for long-distance passenger flights. They give smoother and faster rides than planes with propellers. A single "jumbo jet" can hold over 400 travelers. Today many airlines have fleets of huge jets to carry people everywhere.

Boeing 707

Douglas DC-8

A view inside a modern jumbo jet

R. INNOCENTI

Fires can start deep in the woods. Airplanes speed fire fighters and their equipment to the blaze.

Sometimes there is a flood or an earthquake. When such a thing happens, supplies to towns and villages may be cut off. Small planes can always get through with food and medicine. They can rush injured people to hospitals.

Small planes do many other useful jobs. Rangers spot forest fires from the air. Fishermen and hunters fly small planes to out-of-the-way places. Some of today's cowboys ride airplanes on roundups.

Seaplanes loaded with emergency supplies land in flooded areas.

Rescue planes search for people lost on mountains.

Farmers use small planes to spray their crops against diseases. In Canada and other places where snowfalls are very heavy, planes drop bales of hay to hungry animals. Where homes and ranches are far apart, doctors and veterinarians may make house calls in small planes.

"Crop duster" planes can spray large fields quickly.

Some doctors' planes are like hospitals on wings.

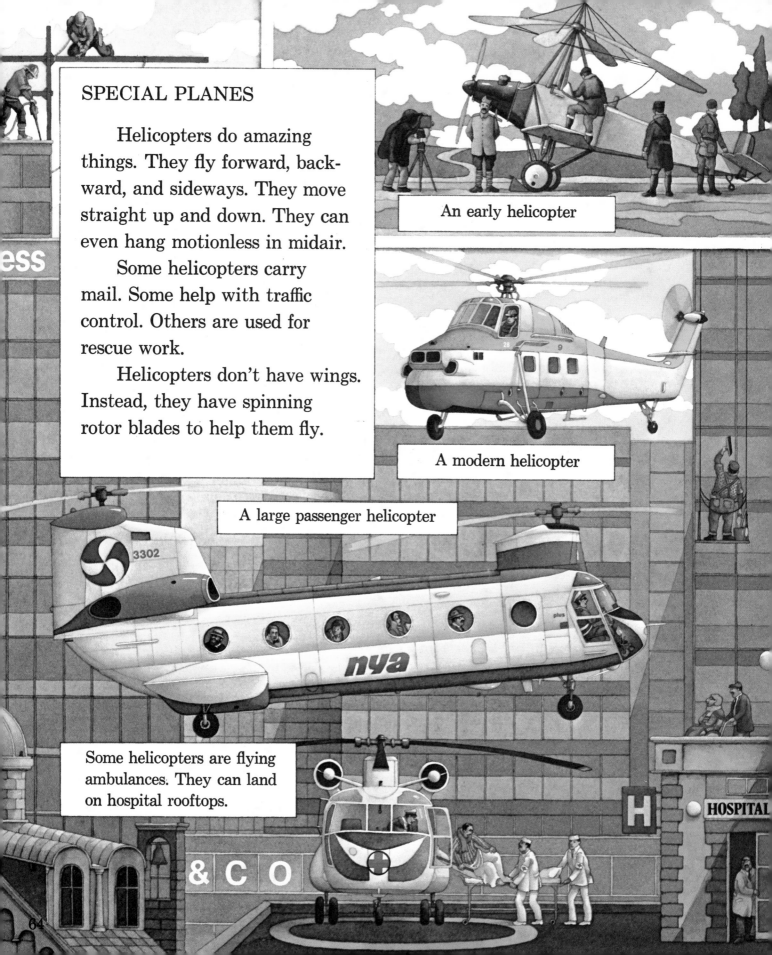

SPECIAL PLANES

Helicopters do amazing things. They fly forward, backward, and sideways. They move straight up and down. They can even hang motionless in midair.

Some helicopters carry mail. Some help with traffic control. Others are used for rescue work.

Helicopters don't have wings. Instead, they have spinning rotor blades to help them fly.

An early helicopter

A modern helicopter

A large passenger helicopter

Some helicopters are flying ambulances. They can land on hospital rooftops.

HOSPITAL

64

These modern aircraft are like those used by the earliest fliers.

Aircraft are also used for fun and sport. Gliders are lightweight planes that do not have engines. They float on currents of air. "Hang gliders" float on air, too. A hang glider looks like a giant wing or kite. The flier hangs underneath it.

Helicopters are also called "choppers" or "whirlybirds."

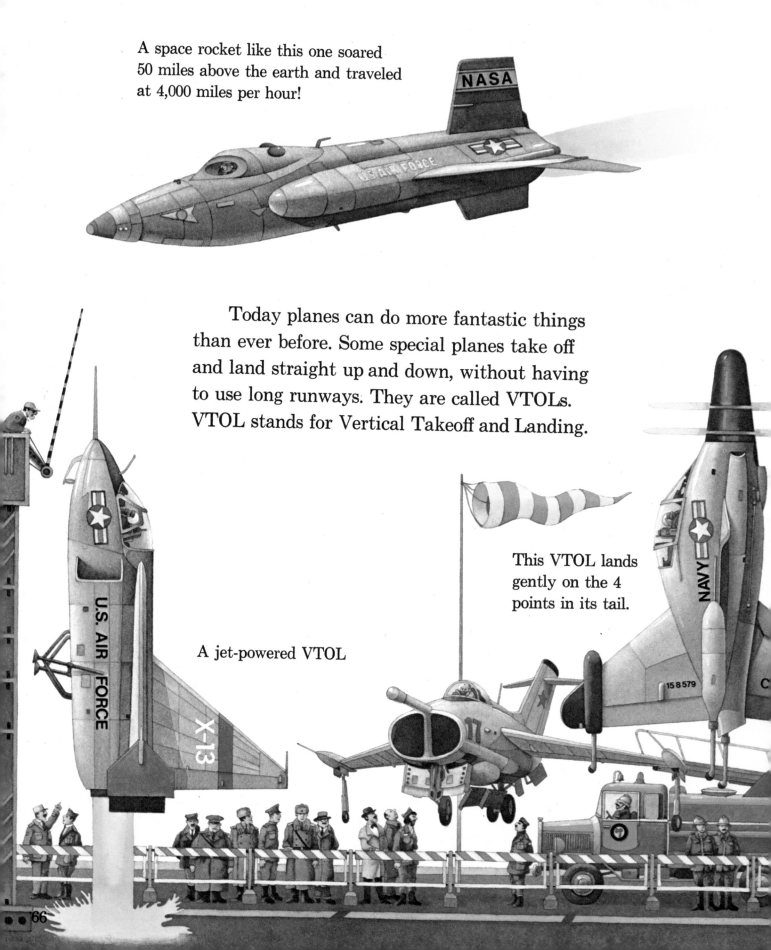

A space rocket like this one soared 50 miles above the earth and traveled at 4,000 miles per hour!

Today planes can do more fantastic things than ever before. Some special planes take off and land straight up and down, without having to use long runways. They are called VTOLs. VTOL stands for Vertical Takeoff and Landing.

A jet-powered VTOL

This VTOL lands gently on the 4 points in its tail.

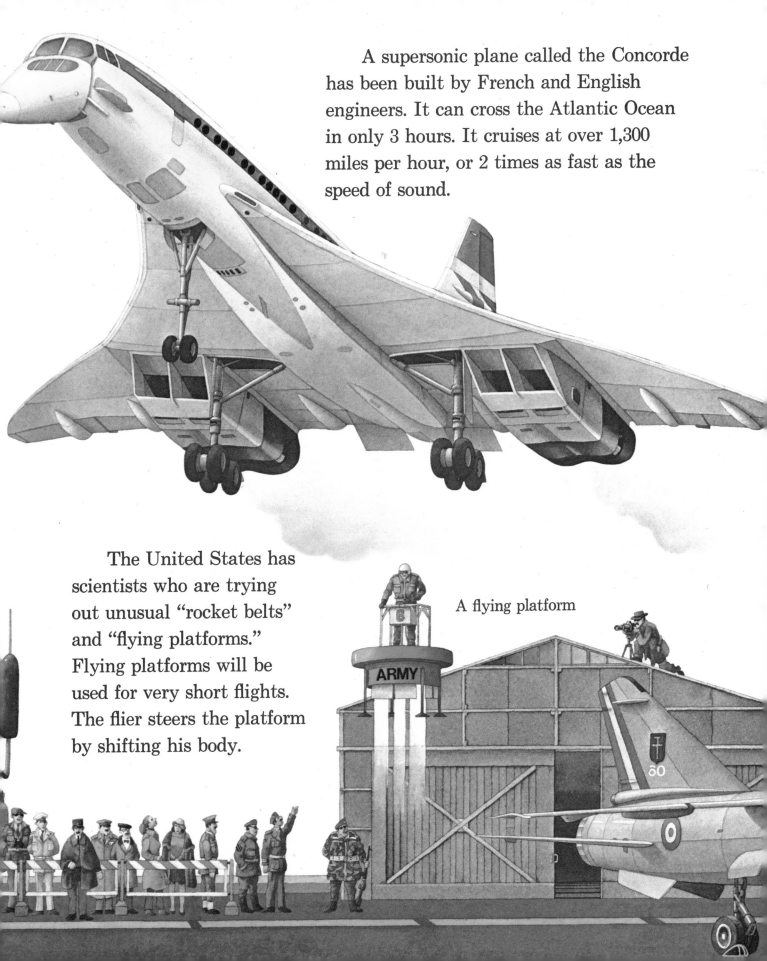

A supersonic plane called the Concorde has been built by French and English engineers. It can cross the Atlantic Ocean in only 3 hours. It cruises at over 1,300 miles per hour, or 2 times as fast as the speed of sound.

The United States has scientists who are trying out unusual "rocket belts" and "flying platforms." Flying platforms will be used for very short flights. The flier steers the platform by shifting his body.

A flying platform

BOEING 747

Number of passengers: 350-450
Number of engines: 4
Cruising speed: 600 miles per hour
Distance of plane from nose to tail: 232 feet

WRIGHT BROTHERS' PLANE

Number of passengers: 1
Number of engines: 1
Cruising speed: 31 miles per hour
Distance covered by first flight: 120 feet

WE'VE COME A LONG WAY

Look up at the sky. Wait a moment or two, and chances are you'll see an airplane fly by. Right this minute, there are hundreds of planes flying to places all over the world.

Since the Wright brothers, there have been many wondrous changes in air travel—changes that have come very fast. Here's a fact that sums it all up: From its nose to its tail, the modern jumbo jet is much longer than the entire distance covered by the Wright brothers in their first flight in 1903!